Multiplication Facts
for the
Dyslexic Student & Visual Learner

Just
the
Facts!

by Cheryl Orlassino

Published by Lulu

For more information visit:
www.help4dyslexia.com

Printed in the United States of America

First Edition
International Standard Book Number (ISBN): 978-0-557-03326-3

Table of Contents

Introduction:

The ideas taught in this book are mainly to give the student memory cues for memorizing the multiplication facts. The student should have an understanding of what it means to multiply (taught in the first section of this book).

Before starting, your student should know the following:

- 12 = 1 Dozen

- 7 days = 1 week
- 14 days = 2 weeks

- February has 28 days.

- 24 hours = 1 day
- 48 hours = 2 days

- Know the double facts (1+1, 2+2, 3+3, etc.)
- Know how to count by 2's, 5's and 10's.

What it means to multiply:

When you see the 'x', think of it as saying:
"groups of".

For example, 2 x 3 means "2 groups of 3".

Below we have two groups of three cookies. Together we have six cookies.

2 x 3 = 6

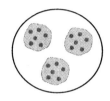 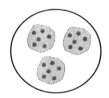

Below we have three groups of two cookies.
Together we have six cookies.
3 x 2 = 6

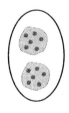 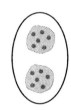 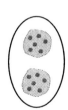

The numbers being multiplied are called **factors** and the total (or answer) is called the **product**. In the above examples, 2 and 3 are the factors and 6 is the product.

     * You can think of it as a **factory (factors)** makes the **product**.

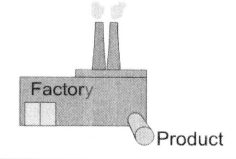

Introducing the Characters

Thirdgrader-3

Sailboat-4

Sammy-6

Sailor-6
(This is Sammy's father)

Daisy-7

Wendy-7
(Daisy's little sister)

Mr. Snowman-8

Mrs. Snowman-8

Snowman-8 Junior

Multiplying by 0

Zero is a magic circle; *any* number to jump into zero will disappear!

$$3 \times 0 = 0$$
$$8 \times 0 = 0$$
$$765 \times 0 = 0$$

Multiplying by 10

To multiply by ten, just add a zero to the number.

Example: 5 x 10 = 5 (add the zero) = 5<u>0</u>

8 x 10 = 8<u>0</u>

6 x 10 = 6<u>0</u>

10 x 4 = 4<u>0</u>

10 x 3 = 3<u>0</u>

12 x 10 = 12<u>0</u>

10 x 11 = 11<u>0</u>

45 x 10 = 45<u>0</u>

10 x 653 = 653<u>0</u>

976,543,219 x 10 = 9,765,432,19<u>0</u>

Multiplying by 1

One is just a plain old mirror; *any* number that stands in front of one will see itself.

$$1 \times \underline{8} = \underline{8}$$

How's my hair?

$$1 \times 2 = 2$$

$$1 \times 3 = 3$$

$$6 \times 1 = 6$$

$$4321 \times 1 = 4321$$

$$987,654,321 \times 1 = 987,654,321$$

Multiplying by 11

Eleven is two ones, so it is two plain old mirrors; *any* number that stands in front of eleven will see itself doubled.

11x <u>8</u> = <u>88</u>

11 x 2 = 22

11 x 3 = 33

6 x 11 = 66

9 x 11 = 99

Multiplying by 9

There are **two** ways to multiply by 9:

Method 1: Using your hands.

Each finger gets a number associated with it (see below).
When you multiply 9 by a number, that numbered finger goes down.
The answer (or product) is the two digit number that is created by
the fingers that are still up. The first digit is to the left of the finger
that's down, and the second digit is to the right of the finger that's down.

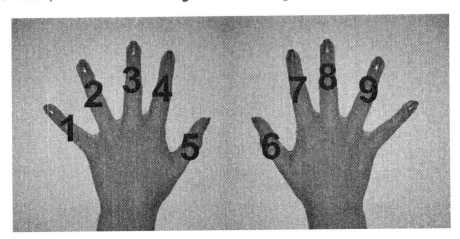

For example: 9 x 3
    The finger with the 3 on it does down
    and the remaining fingers that are still
    up make a 2 (on one side of the finger
    that's down) and a 7 (on the other side).
    Put those digits together and you get 27.
                    9 x 3 = 27

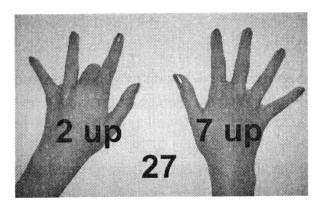

1 x 9 = 9

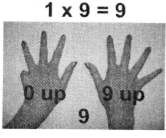

1st finger is down

2 x 9 = 18

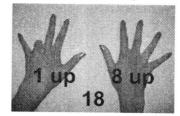

2nd finger is down

3 x 9 = 27

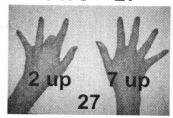

3rd finger is down

4 x 9 = 36

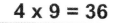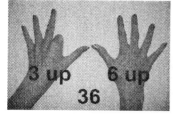

4th finger is down

5 x 9 = 45

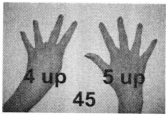

5th finger is down

6 x 9 = 54

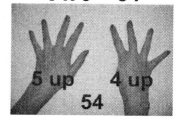

6th finger is down

7 x 9 = 63

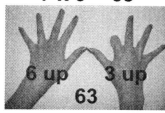

7th finger is down

8 x 9 = 72

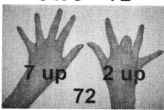

8th finger is down

9 x 9 = 81

9th finger is down

Method 2: Using the factors

This way is very easy, and you don't need two hands to do it.

Step 1: Subtract one from the factor (the one that isn't 9), write it down.

Step2: Starting at that number, count up until you get to nine;
write that number down and there's your answer!

Example: 9 x 7 =

Take one from the seven and write down: **6**

Then count up from 6 to 9 to get 3, write that number down: **63**

And there's your answer: 63

Three Times Facts

3 x 0 = 0	When three jumps in the hole, it disappears.
3 x 1 = 3	When three looks in the mirror it sees a '3'
3 x 2 = 6	Double the three to get six.
3 x 3 = 9	3, 6, 9 it's just a rhyme, to know 3 times 3, say the rhyme 3, 6, 9!
3 x 4 = 12	Thirdgrader-3 and Sailboat-4 went to the baker's to buy 12 donuts for the birthday party (that's *one* dozen donuts)
3 x 5 = 15	Count by 5's.
3 x 6 = 18	Thirdgrader-3 and Sammy-6 take bus 18 to school.
3 x 7 = 21	Thirdgrader-3 has a crush on Daisy-7 and gave her two chocolate hearts and one card for Valentine's Day.
3 x 8 = 24	Snowman-8 Junior eats 3 snow cones every 24 hours (that's one day).
3 x 9 = 27	Use method 1 (hands) or use method 2 (factors).
3 x 10 = 30	Count by 10's or add a zero to the 3 to make 30.

$$3 \times 3 = 9$$

3, 6, 9 it's just a rhyme, to know 3 times 3,
say the rhyme 3, 6, 9!

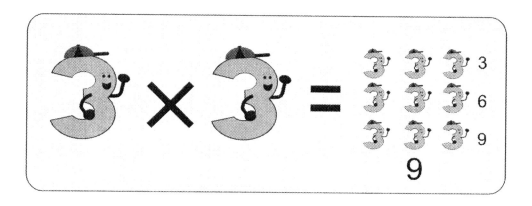

$$3 \times 4 = 12$$

Thirdgrader-3 and Sailboat-4 went to the baker's to buy 12 donuts for the birthday party.

12 Donuts

12

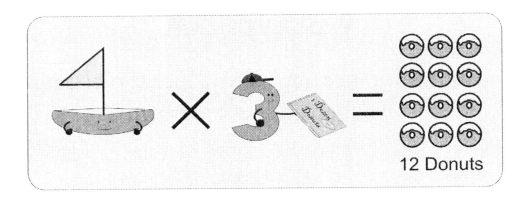

12 Donuts

$$3 \times 6 = 18$$

Thirdgrader-3 and Sammy-6 take
Bus 18 to school.

Bus 18
18

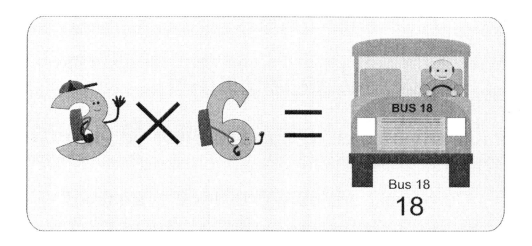

3 x 7 = 21

Thirdgrader-3 has a crush on Daisy-7 and gave her two chocolate hearts and one card for Valentine's Day.

2 Hearts   1 Card

21

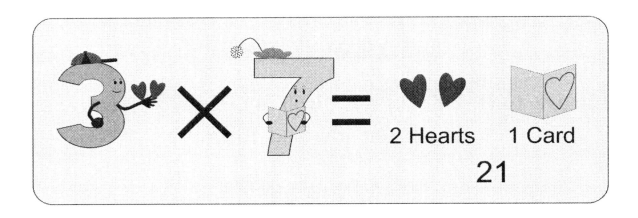

$$3 \times 8 = 24$$

Snowman-8 Junior eats 3 snow cones every 24 hours (that's one day).

 in one day (24 hours)
24

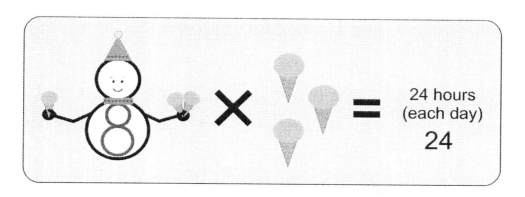

Four Times Facts

4 x 0 = 0	When four jumps in the hole, it disappears.
4 x 1 = 4	When four looks in the mirror it sees a '4'.
4 x 2 = 8	Double the four to get 8.
4 x 3 = 12	Thirdgrader-3 and Sailboat-4 went to the baker's to buy 12 donuts for the birthday party.
4 x 4 = 16	Sailboat-4 and his twin sailed a 16 second race.
4 x 5 = 20	Count by 5's to get 20.
4 x 6 = 24	Sailboat-4 and Sailor-6 sailed for 24 hours (one whole day).
4 x 7 = 28	Sailboat-4 and Daisy-7 go on a cruise for 28 days in February.
4 x 8 = 32	Hungry four ate (eight) three and two (32) - 4 "8" 3 & 2.
4 x 9 = 36	Use method 1 (hands) or use method 2 (factors).
4 x 10 = 40	Count by 10's or add a zero to the 4 to make 40.

4 x 4 = 16

Sailboat-4 and his twin sailed a 16 second race.

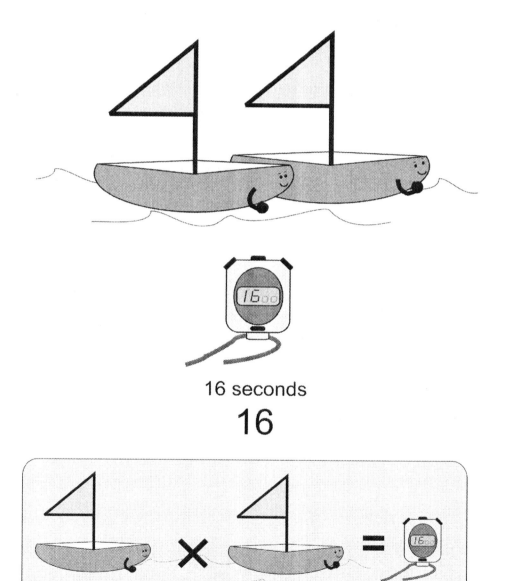

16 seconds

16

$$4 \times 6 = 24$$

Sailboat-4 and Sailor-6 sailed for 24 hours (one whole day).

24 hours
24

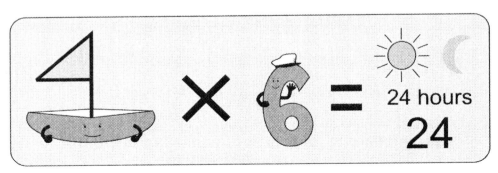

4 x 7 = 28

Sailboat-4 and Daisy-7 go on a cruise for 28 days in February.

28 days

28

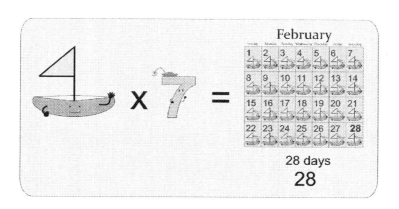

$$4 \times 8 = 32$$

Hungry four ate (eight) his neighbors three and two (32).
Say: 4 "8" 32

___

before: 4 3 2 1

after: 4 _ _ 1

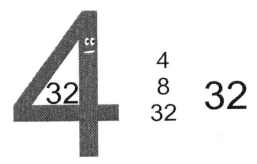

4
8
32   32

$$4 \times 8 = 32$$

Six Times Facts

6 x 0 = 0	When six jumps in the hole, it disappears.
6 x 1 = 6	When six looks in the mirror it sees a '6'.
6 x 2 = 12	Double the 6 to get 12.
6 x 3 = 18	Thirdgrader-3 and Sammy-6 take bus 18 to school.
6 x 4 = 24	Sailboat-6 and Sailor-4 sailed for 24 hours (one whole day).
6 x 5 = 30	Count by 5's.
6 x 6 = 36	Sailor-6 and Sammy-6 go fishing and catch 36 fish.
6 x 7 = 42	Sammy-6 and Daisy-7 had 4 cookies and drank 2 glasses of milk for snack at school.
6 x 8 = 48	Sammy-6 and Snowman-8 Junior went on a ski trip for 48 hours (that's 2 days).
6 x 9 = 54	Use method 1 (hands) or use method 2 (factors).
6 x 10 = 60	Count by 10's or add a zero to the 6 to make 60.

6 x 6 = 36

Sailor-6 and Sammy-6 go fishing and catch 36 fish.

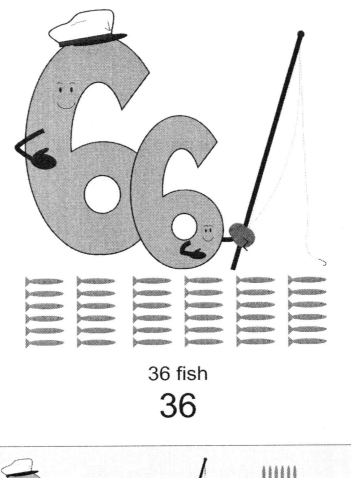

36 fish

36

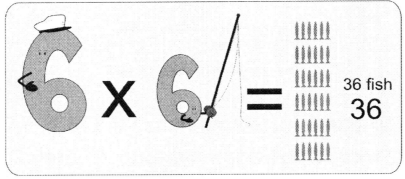

6 x 7 = 42

Sammy-6 and Daisy-7 had 4 cookies and drank 2 glasses of milk for snack at school.

4 Cookies   2 Glasses of Milk

42

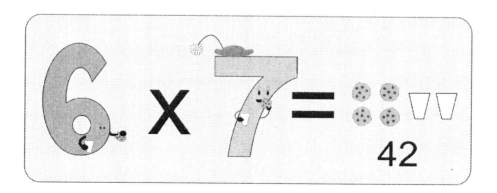

6 x 8 = 48

Sammy-6 and Snowman-8 Junior went on a ski trip for 48 hours (that's 2 days).

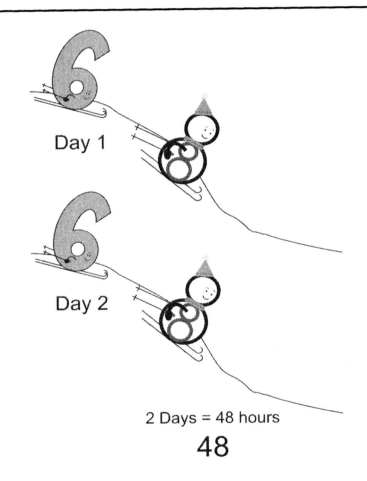

Day 1

Day 2

2 Days = 48 hours

48

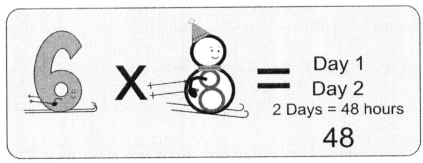

Seven Times Facts

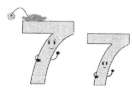

$7 \times 0 = 0$	When seven jumps in the hole, it disappears.
$7 \times 1 = 7$	When seven looks in the mirror it sees a '7'.
$7 \times 2 = 14$	Two weeks is 14 days.
$7 \times 3 = 21$	Thirdgrader-3 has a crush on Daisy-7 and gave her two chocolate hearts and one card for Valentine's Day
$7 \times 4 = 28$	Sailboat-4 and Daisy-7 go on a cruise for 28 days in February.
$7 \times 5 = 35$	Count by 5's.
$7 \times 6 = 42$	Sammy-6 and Daisy-7 ate 4 cookies and drank 2 glasses of milk for snack at school.
$7 \times 7 = 49$	Daisy-7 and her sister, Wendy-7, took a walk in the woods and saw 4 raccoons and 9 rabbits.
$7 \times 8 = 56$	Daisy-7 built Snowman-8 Junior and made him 56 inches tall.
$7 \times 9 = 63$	Use hands or method 2.
$7 \times 10 = 70$	Count by 10's or add a zero to the 7 to make 70.

$$7 \times 2 = 14$$

Two weeks is 14 days.

February

	Sunday	Monday	Tuesday	Wednesday	Thursday	Friday	Saturday
week 1 →	1	2	3	4	5	6	7
week 2 →	8	9	10	11	12	13	14 ♥
	15	16	17	18	19	20	21
	22	23	24	25	26	27	28

2 x 7 days = 14 days

2 x 7 = 14

14

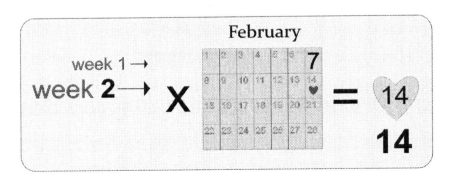

7 x 7 = 49

Daisy-7 and her sister, Wendy-7, took a walk in the woods and saw 4 raccoons and 9 rabbits.

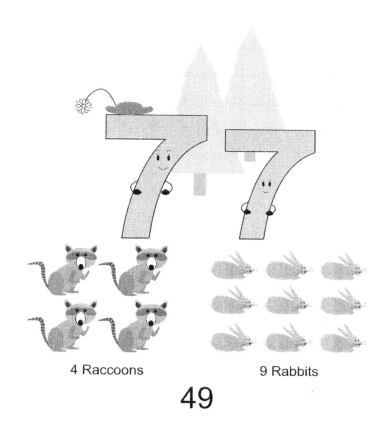

4 Raccoons   9 Rabbits

49

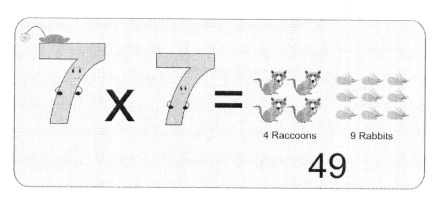

4 Raccoons   9 Rabbits

49

7 x 8 = 56

Daisy-7 built Snowman-8 Junior
and made him 56 inches tall.

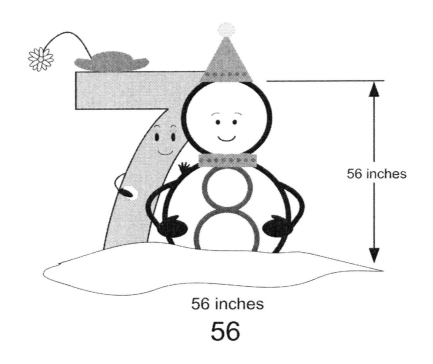

56 inches

56

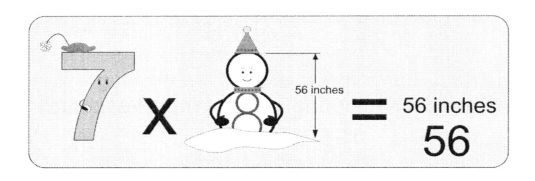

Eight Times Facts

8 x 0 = 0	When eight jumps in the hole, it disappears.
8 x 1 = 8	When eight looks in the mirror it sees another '8'.
8 x 2 = 16	Double the eight to get 16.
8 x 3 = 24	Snowman-8 Junior eats 3 snow cones every 24 hours (that's one day).
8 x 4 = 32	Hungry four ate (eight) three and two (32) - 4 "8" 3&2.
8 x 5 = 40	Count by 5's.
8 x 6 = 48	Sammy-6 and Snowman-8 Junior went on a ski trip for 48 hours (that's 2 days).
8 x 7 = 56	Daisy-7 built Snowman-8 Junior and made him 56 inches tall.
8 x 8 = 64	Mr. Snowman-8 and Mrs. Snowman-8 went to a restaurant for dinner. They ate 6 snow cones and drank 4 Frosties.
8 x 9 = 72	Use method 1 (hands) or use method 2 (factors).
8 x 10 = 80	Count by 10's or add a zero to the 8 to make 80.

8 x 8 = 64

Mr. Snowman-8 and Mrs. Snowman-8 went to a restaurant for dinner. They ate 6 snow cones and drank 4 Frosties.

6 Snow Cones   4 Frosties

64

Multiplication Practice

Cover up the answers and see if you remember them.

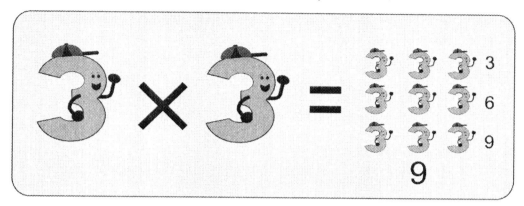

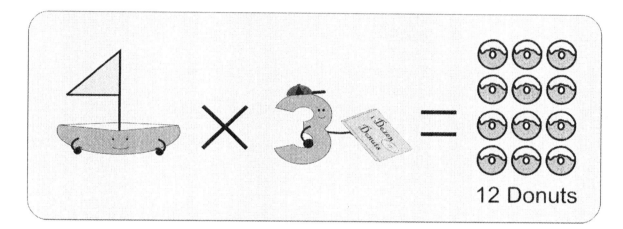

12 Donuts

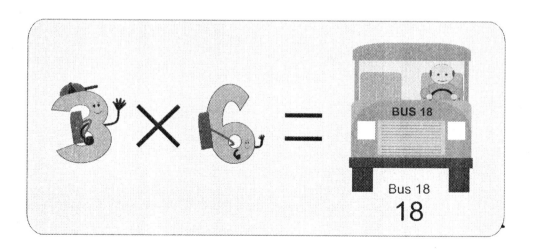

Bus 18

18

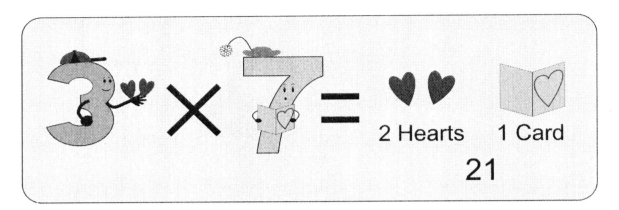

3 × 7 = 2 Hearts   1 Card
21

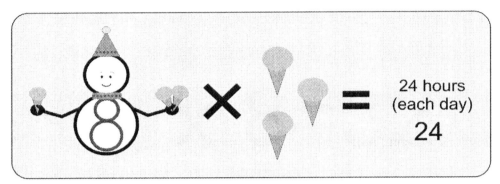

8 × = 24 hours
(each day)
24

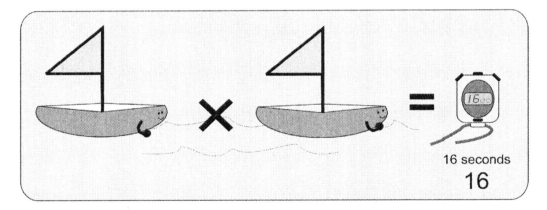

4 × 4 = 16 seconds
16

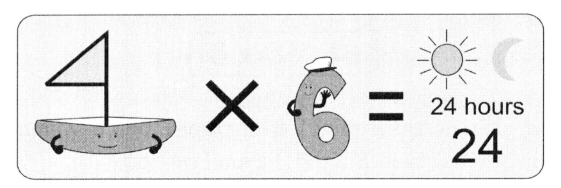

4 × 6 = 24 hours
24

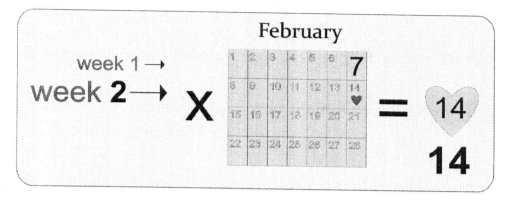

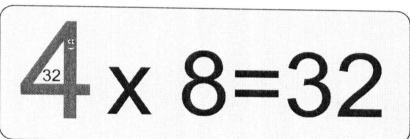

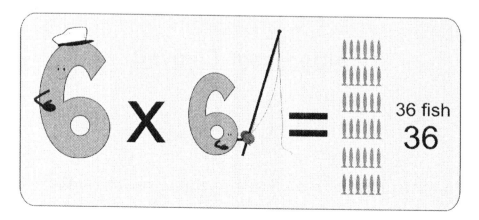

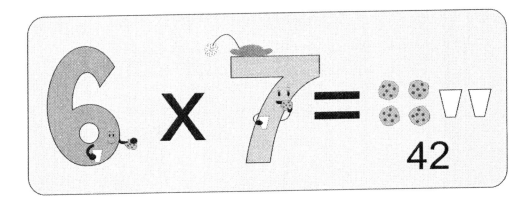

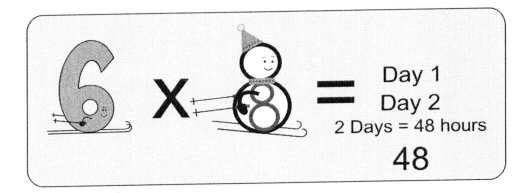

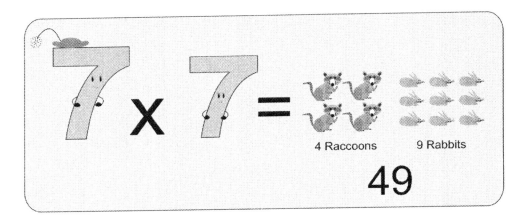

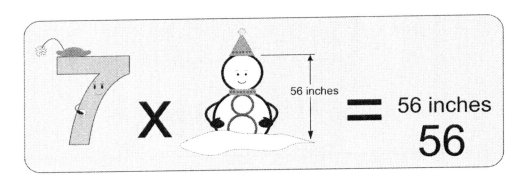

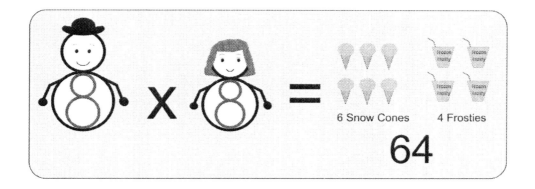

The Commutative Property

The **commutative property** of multiplication means it does not matter which number is first, the answer is the same.

Think of the word "commuter" - A commuter is a person who commutes to work. That means that he or she travels to work. Just like a commuter the factors can change their places and commute to the other side of the multiplication sign.

For example: $3 \times 4 = 12$

The factors, 3 and 4 want to switch places,
so they "commute" to their new spot to become:

$4 \times 3 = 12$

The answer is always 12.

The following equations are for practice. They are the same practice equations as just shown, but they use the **commutative property** to switch the factors around. This will give you practice remembering the math facts regardless of what factor is first.

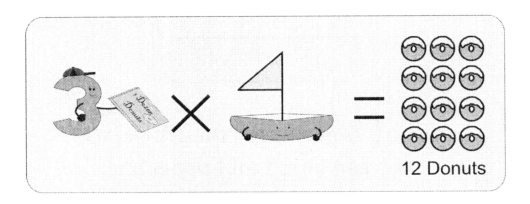

12 Donuts

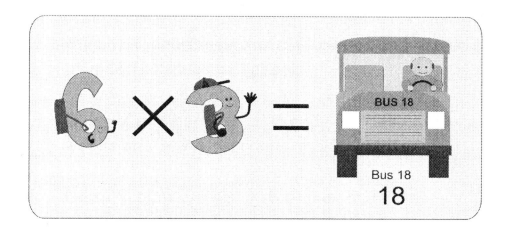

$6 \times 3 = 18$

Bus 18
18

$7 \times 3 = 21$

2 Hearts   1 Card
21

$3 \times 8 = 24$

24 hours
(each day)
24

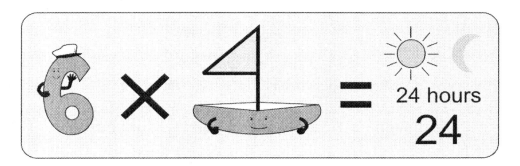

$6 \times 4 = 24$

24 hours
24

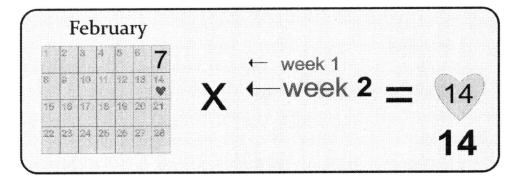

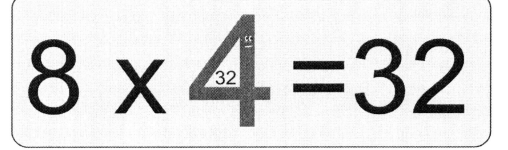

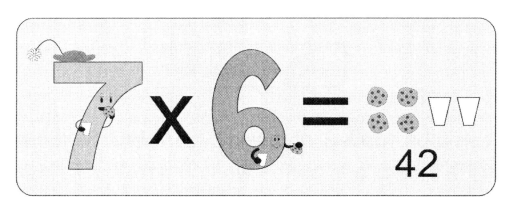

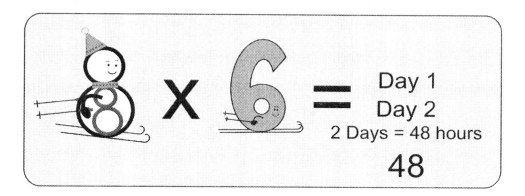

Day 1
Day 2
2 Days = 48 hours
48

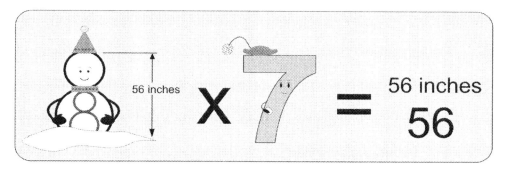

56 inches
56

88

The Associative Property

The **associative property** means that when multiplying, it does not matter how the factors are grouped together, the product (the answer) will be the same. This is true for addition too; however, this is NOT true for subtraction or division.

Think of the word "associate". You associate with your friends and your family. Here we have Sammy-6 and Thirdgrader-3 associating inside parentheses; in the next equation we have Thirdgrader-3 associating with Daisy-7. Either way, the product (the answer) is 126.

$$(6 \times 3) \times 7 = 126$$

$$6 \times (3 \times 7) = 126$$

$$(6 \times 3) \times 7 = 126$$

$$6 \times (3 \times 7) = 126$$

Practice With Vertical Multiplication Problems

X

_____

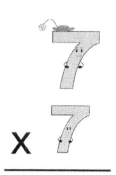

X

_____

X

_____

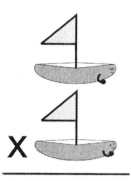

X

_____

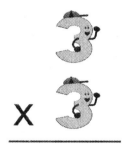

X

_____

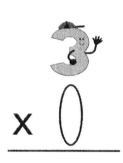

X

_____

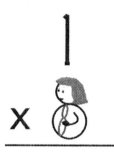

X

_____

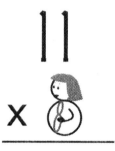

X

_____

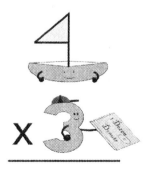

X

_____

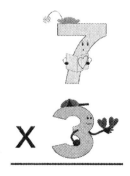

X

_____

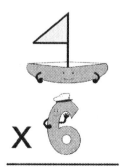

X

_____

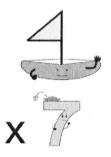

X

_____

$\begin{array}{r} 4 \\ \times\ 8 \\ \hline \end{array}$

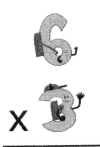

$\begin{array}{r} 6 \\ \times\ 3 \\ \hline \end{array}$

$\begin{array}{r} 6 \\ \times\ 7 \\ \hline \end{array}$

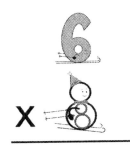

$\begin{array}{r} 6 \\ \times\ 8 \\ \hline \end{array}$

$\begin{array}{r} 7 \\ \times\quad \\ \hline \end{array}$

$\begin{array}{r} 8 \\ \times\ 3 \\ \hline \end{array}$

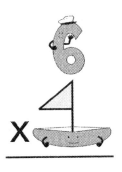

$\begin{array}{r} 6 \\ \times\ 4 \\ \hline \end{array}$

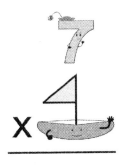

$\begin{array}{r} 7 \\ \times\ 4 \\ \hline \end{array}$

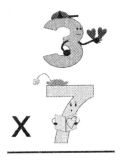

$\begin{array}{r} 3 \\ \times\ 7 \\ \hline \end{array}$

$\begin{array}{r} 8 \\ \times\ 4 \\ \hline \end{array}$

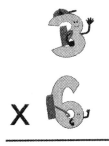

$\begin{array}{r} 3 \\ \times\ 6 \\ \hline \end{array}$

$\begin{array}{r} 3 \\ \times\ 4 \\ \hline \end{array}$

Name the missing numbers:

8 × ? = 64

7 × ? = 49

6 × ? = 36

4 × ? = 16

3 × ? = 9

3 × ? = 0

1 × ? = 8

11 × ? = 88

4 × ? = 12

7 × ? = 21

4 × ? = 24

4 × ? = 28

$$\begin{array}{r} 4 \\ \times\ ? \\ \hline 32 \end{array} \qquad \begin{array}{r} ? \\ \times\ 3 \\ \hline 18 \end{array} \qquad \begin{array}{r} ? \\ \times\ 7 \\ \hline 42 \end{array} \qquad \begin{array}{r} 6 \\ \times\ ? \\ \hline 48 \end{array}$$

$$\begin{array}{r} ? \\ \times\ \\ \hline 56 \end{array} \qquad \begin{array}{r} 8 \\ \times\ ? \\ \hline 24 \end{array} \qquad \begin{array}{r} 6 \\ \times\ ? \\ \hline 24 \end{array} \qquad \begin{array}{r} 7 \\ \times\ ? \\ \hline 49 \end{array}$$

$$\begin{array}{r} ? \\ \times\ 7 \\ \hline 21 \end{array} \qquad \begin{array}{r} ? \\ \times\ 4 \\ \hline 32 \end{array} \qquad \begin{array}{r} ? \\ \times\ 6 \\ \hline 18 \end{array} \qquad \begin{array}{r} 3 \\ \times\ ? \\ \hline 12 \end{array}$$

Final Multiplication Practice

8 x 3 =	3 x 0 =	10 x 5 =
4 x 6 =	5 x 1 =	4 x 10 =
0 x 3 =	2 x 8 =	5 x 3 =
3 x 3 =	9 x 3 =	8 x 5 =
6 x 3 =	9 x 0 =	9 x 2 =
7 x 3 =	11 x 4 =	10 x 8 =
4 x 4 =	7 x 2 =	5 x 9 =
1 x 8 =	6 x 1 =	5 x 5 =
2 x 7 =	9 x 8 =	10 x 10 =
6 x 7 =	6 x 2 =	11 x 10 =
8 x 6 =	0 x 1 =	5 x 4 =
8 x 7 =	7 x 9 =	2 x 8 =
6 x 6 =	2 x 4 =	5 x 6 =
7 x 8 =	7 x 0 =	9 x 5 =
8 x 4 =	1 x 3 =	3 x 2 =
4 x 7 =	6 x 11 =	5 x 0 =
7 x 7 =	8 x 2 =	8 x 5 =
8 x 8 =	9 x 9 =	10 x 8 =
7 x 6 =	2 x 5 =	7 x 5 =
3 x 8 =	9 x 2 =	10 x 4 =
4 x 6 =	5 x 9 =	3 x 5 =

Division

Division is the opposite of multiplication, just like subtraction is the opposite of addition. For multiplying, the 'x' means 'groups of'. For division the symbol '÷' tells you to split the number into equal groups.

For example:
If you had 4 friends and you wanted to divide 12 apples so that each friend gets an equal amount, then you would divide up the 12 apples into 4 equal groups. Each friend would get 3 apples.

$$12 \div 4 = 3$$

Here we are dividing 12 into 4 equal groups of 3:

12 apples   4 groups   3 apples for each group

For multiplication, we have **factors** (the numbers being multiplied) and the product (the answer). For division, we also have special names for the numbers; they are **'dividend'**, **'divisor'** and **'quotient'**.

$$12 \div 4 = 3$$

dividend   divisor   quotient

There are three ways to write out a division problem:

$$12 \div 4 = 3 \qquad \frac{12}{4} = 3 \qquad 4\overline{)12}\,^{3}$$

To remember the names:

Dividend: divid**end** has the word '**end**' in it. This number is the group that will be divided up. In other words, the larger group is coming to an **end**.

Divisor: divis**or** has the word '**or**' in it, which starts the word '**or**ganize'. This is the number that says how many equal groups you get, or how many groups are being **or**ganized.

Quotient: **qu**otient starts with a '**qu**' just like the word '**qu**estion'. The **qu**otient is the answer to the **qu**estion.

To remember where the numbers go:

It's easy to get confused with where the numbers go for division. To make it easy to remember, think of a chopping block. The chopping block is where the dividend (the number to be divided up) goes to get... er, chopped up. Gulp!

$$12 \div 4 = 3$$

When written in this form, the first number on the left gets chopped up (or divided).

$$\frac{12}{4} = 3$$

When written in this form, the line is the chopping block and anything that goes on the chopping block will get chopped up (or divided).

$$4 \overline{)12}^{\,3}$$

When written in this form, the number caught inside the box (well, it's sort of like a box) will get chopped up (or divided).

- 51 -

To Check Your Answer:

Since division is the opposite of multiplication, you can check your answer by multiplying the answer (the quotient) with the divisor to see if it equals the dividend (the number that got divided).

Below shows the three forms of division. To check your answer, multiply the numbers that are circled:

$$12 \div 4 = 3 \qquad \frac{12}{4} = 3 \qquad 4\overline{)12}\,^3$$

Division Practice:

12 donuts

$$12 \div 4 = ?$$

2 mirrors

$$88 \div 11 = ?$$

24 hours or 1 day

$$24 \div 8 = ?$$

2 Hearts   1 Card

$$21 \div 7 = ?$$

Bus 18

$$18 \div 6 = ?$$

1 mirror

$$8 \div 1 = ?$$

Say the rhyme...

$$9 \div 3 = ?$$

4 Raccoons & 9 Rabbits

$$49 \div 7 = ?$$

2 Hearts   1 Card

$$21 \div 3 = ?$$

4 Cookies   2 Glasses of Milk

$$42 \div 6 = ?$$

16 seconds

$$16 \div 4 = ?$$

48 hours or 2 days

$$48 \div 6 = ?$$

Division Practice

6 Snow Cones   4 Frosties

$$\frac{64}{8} = ?$$

12 donuts

$$\frac{12}{4} = ?$$

Bus 18

$$\frac{18}{6} = ?$$

24 hours or 1 day trip

$$\frac{24}{4} = ?$$

4 Cookies   2 Glasses of Milk
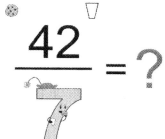

$$\frac{42}{7} = ?$$

24 hours or 1 day

$$\frac{24}{8} = ?$$

28 day trip

$$\frac{28}{4} = ?$$

$$\frac{32}{4} = ?$$

56 inches

$$\frac{56}{7} = ?$$

2 Hearts   1 Card

$$\frac{21}{7} = ?$$

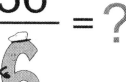
36 fish

$$\frac{36}{6} = ?$$

2 Days or 48 hours
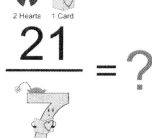

$$\frac{48}{8} = ?$$

Just the Facts!

4 Raccoons   9 Rabbits

$$\frac{49}{7} = ?$$

$$\frac{14}{2} = ?$$

4 Cookies   2 Glasses of Milk
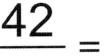

$$\frac{42}{6} = ?$$

56 inches

$$\frac{56}{?} = ?$$
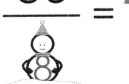

2 Hearts   1 Card

$$\frac{21}{3} = ?$$

28 day trip

$$\frac{28}{7} = ?$$

Say the rhyme..

$$\frac{9}{3} = ?$$

24 hours or 1 day trip

$$\frac{24}{6} = ?$$

12 donuts

$$\frac{12}{3} = ?$$

16 seconds

$$\frac{16}{4} = ?$$

2 Days or 48 hours

$$\frac{48}{6} = ?$$

Bus 18

$$\frac{18}{3} = ?$$

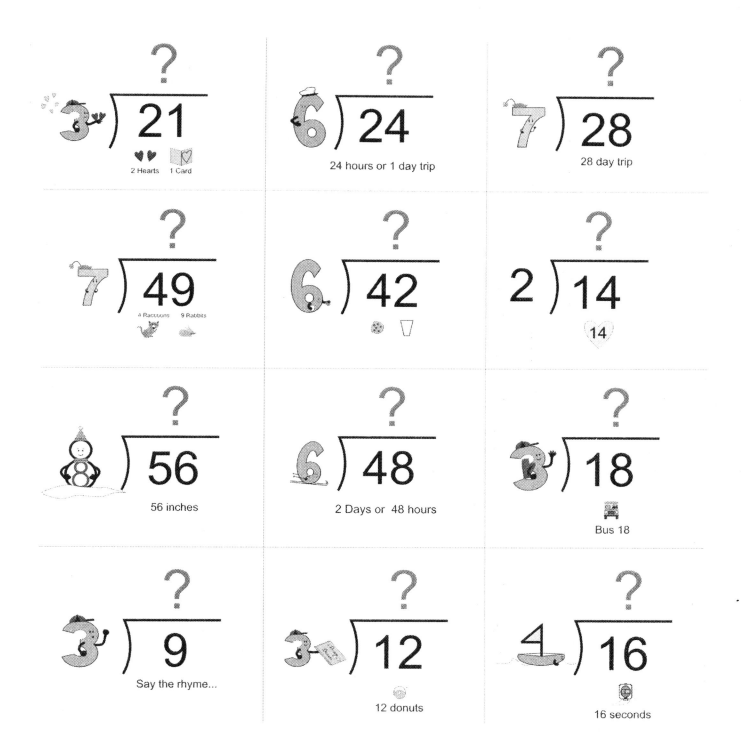

? / 21
2 Hearts 1 Card

? / 24
24 hours or 1 day trip

? / 28
28 day trip

? / 49
4 Raccoons 9 Rabbits

? / 42

? / 14
14

? / 56
56 inches

? / 48
2 Days or 48 hours

? / 18
Bus 18

? / 9
Say the rhyme...

? / 12
12 donuts

? / 16
16 seconds

? 8)48
2 Days or 48 hours

? 7)56
56 inches

? 6)36
36 fish

? 6)18
Bus 18

? 8)24
24 hours or 1 day

? 8)64
6 Snow Cones   4 Frosties

? 4)12
12 donuts

? 7)42
4 Cookies   2 Glasses of Milk

? 4)24
24 hours or 1 day trip

? 4)28
28 day trip

? 4)32

? 7)21
2 Hearts   1 Card